hurting heart

LILLIAN VILLARRUEL

WWW.13THANDJOAN.COM

Hurting Heart. Copyright 2019 by Lillian Villarruel. All rights reserved. No part of this publication may be reproduced, distributed, or transmitted in any form or by any means, including photocopying, recording, or other electronic or mechanical methods, without the prior written permission of the publisher, except in the case of brief quotations embodied in critical reviews and certain other noncommercial uses permitted by copyright law. For permission requests, write to the publisher, addressed "Attention: Permissions Coordinator," 500 N. Michigan Avenue, Suite #600, Chicago, IL 60611.

13th & Joan books may be purchased for educational, business or sales promotional use. For information, please email the Sales Department at sales@13thandjoan.com.

ISBN: 978-1-7335154-9-8

Dedication

This book is dedicated to all the women who needed their father and to every girl who looked for him in every man.
To all the women who still have that little girl in them that yearns for his love and those who cried themselves to sleep, wondering why they weren't good enough.
To all the women who have struggled with relationships emotionally and physically.
To all the women who have trust issues because of feelings of abandonment.
To all the women who have wondered how confident they would be as a woman if their dad had only been present.
To all the women who just wanted to feel loved.
To all who just want to find home in someone.
To all the women who have been torn apart and broken into pieces... but are still standing.
This one's for you.

And lastly,
To my sweet mother.
There are no words that could ever describe
how a precious of an angel you are.
Thank you for everything you did for us.
I love you more than you'll ever know.

LILLIAN VILLARRUEL

When my heart hurts, my mind forgets.
So, i write to remember

i needed the pain in order to feel
i needed the pain in order to write
so i thank you for feeding off my light.

Letters to my father

-Dear Dad, i've searched for your love everywhere. Even in you. And i still can't find it.

-Dear Dad, you were the first man to ever break my heart.

-Dad, it is the most unsettling feeling to know i have a father but you're not here. i needed you to help form the strong woman in me. But instead i had to make myself. Why am i mourning you?
You are alive.
You once told me that the way to keep a person alive is by never forgetting them and thinking about them every day.
Well, why didn't you think of me?
Because i'm sure i feel anything but alive.

HURTING HEART

-To my dearest father,
it breaks my heart knowing that i have spoken to
you my whole life about nothing in particular
and i have never known who you really are.
i will miss you the most,
because i never got a chance to live in your heart.
i lay awake at night and cry.
i long for a love so deep, that it cures my hurt.
A fatherly love that is.

Don't be afraid of the dark

No one can see me in this darkness. No
one bothers to tell me to come home.
No one bothered
to give me their hand and pull me up.
SEE ME!
Why can't you see me?
But wait,
It's me that needs to see. Can't you
see that all this darkness is
What lead you to your happenings. Can't
you see that without the terrible darkness,
THERE IS NO YOU.

HURTING HEART

Life

In a room full of people,
i'm surrounded by this feeling of loneliness.
Why does this hurt so much?

LILLIAN VILLARRUEL

You knew i'd never tell.
You probably think i don't remember.
Maybe i was too little to understand.
So, you pretend it never happened.
But the thing is i do remember.
You touched me in places that you told me were to
remain sacred.
And you were right, i didn't understand.
But i knew i didn't like it.
You had no right.
And up until now, i have screamed
without a sound.

HURTING HEART

As i sit at the table trying to act normal
i am filled with one of the worst feelings,
trying to eat my dinner while swallowing back
tears.
There was nothing more hurtful
than a fake family dinner.

LILLIAN VILLARRUEL

How he tries to keep me

i love you, but i'm falling for her. -him

Insecurity

i stare at her pictures making my mind
believe that she is the most beautiful
woman because you want her.
i try my best to steal her look.
What was it in her that you didn't see in me.
i was so empty and felt so lost. Or
maybe i was lost in her,
because maybe if i was just like her, you'd want me
just as much.

You're not here

Thoughts of her get lost between my legs and
thighs.
Your eyes are glossy and i begin to wonder
If you even know it's me you're making love to.

HURTING HEART

i hope that one day you realize that i
was the only one who genuinely cared.
i just know that by the time you realize it,
i will have come to my senses and moved on.

LILLIAN VILLARRUEL

Never mix a broken heart with a full glass,
You'll end up tearing yourself apart.

HURTING HEART

When you left,
i told stories to the wind about our love,
so everyday it would whisper memories of us
and haunt you forever.

LILLIAN VILLARRUEL

The stars knew how much love i held for you
i used to talk to them about you.
The moon knew your name.
For i spent countless nights crying over you.
And the sun could relate to the warmth in your soul,
But it just always seems to set a little too soon.

HURTING HEART

You heard me, but hardly ever listened.
You talked but would hardly ever speak to me.
And when you touched me you hardly ever felt me.
i have settled for you when you weren't even all in.
i was living with your ghost.

LILLIAN VILLARRUEL

Loving you never hurt so much,
And your touch felt lonelier than ever before,
Having you by my side kept my heart trapped.
i kept looking for heaven in the hell you gave me.

HURTING HEART

i never knew how lonely i was,
till a stranger touched my hand and spoke to me
softly,
i could feel their love.
The type of love that you kept hidden from me.

Sex with you began to mean nothing.
i knew you had begun to make love to her through
me.
And nothing was the same after that.

You'd always say how you only wanted me,
But then your eyes would wander every chance you got.
The world was consuming you, and
you did nothing to stop it.

LILLIAN VILLARRUEL

You didn't want me for me.
You only wanted my love,
But you kept giving it away
And draining every ounce of me
till there was nothing left.

HURTING HEART

Your eyes could never hide anything.
i could see right through you.
they said you would leave me.
And still…. i chose to stay.

i want to keep going,
but i'm oh so tired.
i keep swimming in this shipless sea
And the only thing that keeps me going
Is the thought of one day finding you.

i hate this world that we call home
and i'm pretty sure it hates me as much as i do.
i did all my best to smile and waited for better days.
But they never came, so i continued to slip away.

i love you,
but i feel so lonely when i'm with you.
Why am i not good enough?

i do not belong here
please someone take me away.
Show me the way for i am weary and tired.

i left you a long time ago
but your memories still linger
and your hurt still hurts.

HURTING HEART

There i stood,
Existing but hardly living.
Getting lost in thoughts.
My mind races and i can't find the way out.
i see life around me growing green and fruitful,
but i was stuck in the forgotten.
A place where no one dared to enter.

You'd say you loved me,
But then you wouldn't come home.
And then you wouldn't call.
And i'd wait around wondering why
Fighting my own thoughts.
And when i'd finally gather the strength to move on,
You'd come right back.

HURTING HEART

It happened already,
But you're driving yourself crazy.
Going over details of what he said
Or things he promised he'd never do.
You can't help but talk about it all the time
When you know you need to just let it go.

LILLIAN VILLARRUEL

People had begun to catch on,
They'd ask why i was upset or why
i never seemed to smile.
It was so hard to fake happiness when i
knew that in front of everyone else,
It was all just a show.
They saw you as a great man and
couldn't understand why i was hurt.
You were a great actor.

No one ever took the time to treat her
with the love and respect she deserved.
Now all she had were these bad experi-
ences where men took advantage of her
She never stopped longing for more,
She was a dreamer,
A hopeless romantic,
And she knew that one day she'd meet
the love she always longed for.
She didn't know where. She didn't know when
But she'd never give up.

Trapped

It hurts loving you,
But it hurt much more to leave.

Her

i miss when things were simple,
just me and you.
Now she's tainted the picture and
lingers in the happiness.

Why do you keep me?

Your eyes wander every chance you get,
i sit there smiling telling you stories.
You nod your head but seem disinterested
Your mind is somewhere else imagining what you would
Do to the woman who walks by us.
i stay,
hoping one day you can look at me in the eyes
and smile because you are grateful for my love.

The reason why i kept holding on, was because
Love with you,
Was life.
But it wasn't much of a life worth living,
When i was the only one invested.

Coward

You look the best when you're in
pain you'd say to yourself.
You'd watch me cry, hurt, become vulnerable
You created insecurities in me because you knew
That only in those ways would i love you.
You kept me broken because you
knew that once i was whole,
i'd realize you meant nothing.

When he cheated

Your actions became trends,
Your words began to mean nothing
You were no longer credible and i had become
immune to your selfish ways. Each time making
it easier and easier for me to slip away.

LILLIAN VILLARRUEL

The way you held me,
The way you made me laugh,
The way you loved me,
A love without betrayal was heaven.
Till i remembered…and then,
It was picturing you doing that with her
That cracked my heart down to the very core.

HURTING HEART

Processing the hurt

My heart is crying
My insides are cringing
How can this be real?
How do i make you come back?
If only i could turn back time,
This can't be real.

A perfect illusion,
Like a beautiful dream,
i was in heaven.
i had been wandering as a lonely soul through a desert.
i must've been mistaken for what i thought was real
was only a mirage of how much i desired love
i was now trapped in a nightmare.
Where every time i open my
eyes, it doesn't go away.

HURTING HEART

Time and time again,
They will let you down.
i'll try not to be disappointed,
i'll try not to hurt,
but i'll never be able to understand how a person
can hurt and destroy
the one they love.

You hold me, and my heart says this isn't you
Where have you gone?
Our hearts were fluent, but you could not hear it's cry anymore.
i am drowning in these tears inside me that i have not shed.
There's a knot in my throat,
i can barely breath,
every moment that passes has me going under,
there are no rescue boats in sight.
Just the sound of underwater cries.

Open up

i didn't need to talk,
i needed to feel
Your heart, your energy, your love.
Those feelings told me so much more
than having to ask what was wrong.

LILLIAN VILLARRUEL

There i sat,
With a knot in my throat
Holding back tears,
Smiling but my lips were quivering.
Trapped in a feeling i could not escape.
Silently holding the loudest pain,
How was it possible to keep holding onto something
i could barely carry.

Letting go

i must leave you.
i just don't know if i'm capable of doing it.
i'm scared,
because i know you're not the one.
But just the thought of letting you go
makes my heart ache so much.

Lost cause

i begged you to stay so many times.
i yearned for your affection.
All i wanted was attention.
i couldn't fix it.
After so many times i tried putting it
back together, you still didn't want it.
Until i finally left.

Insanity

i kept going back to you.
Believing your promises.
i kept going back to you, but it was all false hope.
i kept expecting different results
even though i already knew the outcome.
i was insane.

My wish to you

Every night i'd pray.
i'd pray to forget you.
i'd pray to not feel the pain of losing you.
i'd ask God to make me stronger and help me get through this.
But on this particular night, i prayed for you.
i prayed for your heart.
i pray God touches you so deep in your soul.
i have forgiven you, i just hope you forgive me.

i felt like i was hanging on for dear life to you.
Each time slipping away more.
i'm sorry.
i promise that if this is my souls purpose,
and if not in this lifetime,
it will be in the next.
i will find you
and i will love you.
i will take care of you and give you the care that
no one gave you,
i love you, i'm sorry.

You broke me

i was never the same after you.
As much as i tried to act like i was ok.
i wasn't.
you broke me.

Tangled

i've had many short relationships
as a form of survival mode.
Anything that made me feel at
home or wanted i'd take it.
As long as it would get me through the
next period i was going through.
i just wasn't the same after you.

The devil

You broke me in the form of different bodies each time.
But it was you bringing me down.

HURTING HEART

Home is you

Which way is home?
i just want to go home.
Please,
i miss the feeling of home.

LILLIAN VILLARRUEL

Hurting

when sadness overtakes,
why is it that i run back to the people
who made it run through my
veins in the first place?

Past relationships

i go back to you every time.
You and you and you.
Because today i'm searching for home.
Anything and everything that'll give me that fix.
Home is you, and you.

LILLIAN VILLARRUEL

First love

You're never really the same after that first love.
That wild roller-coaster of burning love.
That's the one that kills you.
i feel sorry for anyone who comes after that.

The definition of love
(Domestic violence)

He yells, calls you names.
Creates the insecurity in you.
He kills your spirit.
Controls you and makes you feel worthless.
Then forces himself on you.
Terrified i ask, why?
i love you he says.
This is what love is.

Let down

in those eyes there lies sadness,
hurt, anger, and lies.
You question your whole life.
Maybe this is your destiny.

Myself

i've known you my whole life,
but i still don't know who you are.

Eye opener

When the truth turns out to have
been a lie this whole time,
You start evolving.
You'll never be the same i'll tell you that.

Tired of life

i'm struggling to find my words.
What the hell am i even doing here.

LILLIAN VILLARRUEL

Dancing with the devil

you swore you'd never be like your father,
you hate his ways.
But you still can't help it.
You can't help but love to feel the pain
Because it was all you ever knew.

The love we accept

i deserve better than what you
have been creating for me.

Selfish

Why is it only when i am gone that you realize
i was the one person you should
have invested your time in?

Emptiness

i don't recognize myself anymore.

High school

They stare and whisper and i
pretend not to notice.
The sound of their idiotic laugh-
ter gets under my skin.

Pain

Remembering i still love you.

LILLIAN VILLARRUEL

Born to be the other woman

She didn't care you loved me.
She didn't care i loved you.
She didn't care we had years of history.
She was the other woman.
But little did she know that she
rescued me from you.

Should've known better- a fool

i gave up everything for you.
My family, my friends, everything.
Just to be with you.

LILLIAN VILLARRUEL

Trust

You never caught me each time i fell.
So, i had to learn to fly.

To those i've hurt

To those i've hurt when i was hurting.
i want to apologize,
for my heart was built on lies.

Lost

it took losing my mind to find myself.

Suffering

i fell to my knees,
begging, weeping, embarrassing myself.
While you sat there laughing and
thinking how pathetic i was.
i'm on my knees.
But you wanted me in the dark.
You loved watching me hurt.

Thief

You loved seeing me hurt.
You loved seeing me cry and lose faith in all things.
It gave you this sense of power and you
loved being in control of my life
because you fed off my light.

Unhealthy

Each time you made my heart beat slower,
My pulse weaker,
My eyes blurred with tears of pain.
The ache in my soul was unbearable
i spent a decade on your life support
You were a slow death.

Lessons

Every time you'd fail me
i'd curse the lord for allow-
ing me to cross your path
when the only person i should've
been blaming was myself.
i was just too weak to let you go and the lord
was too strong to let me fail.

Numb

i had become so accustomed to
giving up my body to you,
that i began to offer it in times i needed saving
from your abusive.
i had become numb.

LILLIAN VILLARRUEL

Trying to forget

When i think of you, i think of a distant memory.
i get lost thinking of all the tears i
shed, the abuse i endured.
i don't even know that person
i used to be anymore.

Searching

The way the sun sets,
The way the moon glimmers over the ocean,
The way the wind rustles through leaves on a tree.
All i can think about is how i miss some-
thing i'm not yet sure exists.

Childhood memories

Cover your ears
i can't even hear my thoughts with
all this yelling and screaming.
It's loud in here. My heart is sinking.
i wish i could control all this hatred
and unhappiness between them.
i'm trying to be ok but my voice is cracking.
Cover your ears i tell my brother. Let's
go hide in the closet. it'll all be ok.
i hear thumps against the wall.
Why don't they just stop.
Voices get louder, fear gets stronger
Silence....
Here comes that lonely silence again.
as tears fall, feelings of regret and
unhappiness have arrived.

Your touch felt lonely

In the stillness of the night
Lying next to you,
Knowing you only wanted me for your selfish ways
And for the nights i was convenient.
Just the thought of there being some-
thing more out there just waiting for me,
gave me the most unsettling and lone-
liest feeling having you by my side.

The impossible

letting go of you is impossible.
The more i try to let you go, the
more i remember you.
You were more than just any other thing.
You were my home.

i see you

i can see through your walls that you put up.
i see you through that storm and
those crashing waves.
You have so much potential and that's
why i can't help but still want you.
i wish you'd only just let me love you.

Benefit of the doubt

i was searching for love.
The kind that would fill me up and i
would never know i was hungry for.
i was searching for love while holding
on to something so cruel.
You were so toxic and selfish.
i was accepting so much abuse,
and still saying i wanted love.

Family/friends

They all look at me like i'm crazy.
i pretend like they're wrong and act
accordingly when they're around.
But deep down inside, i know they're right.

LILLIAN VILLARRUEL

Home

i miss the feeling of home.
i miss something i've never had.

You fool

It is only when i am gone
Till you realize i was the one person
You should've invested your time in.

Mornings are the worst

Waking without you,
Is like losing you all over again.
i lose you every day.

HURTING HEART

You were no good for me.
You were hurting my soul.
When i finally remembered my name,
That's when i let you go.

LILLIAN VILLARRUEL

Saving you was the hardest thing,
As the darkness pulled you in,
i held tight begging you not to go.
But you wanted to.
So when it took you,
i was all alone.

A magician

You do something to me.
You make my heartbeat fast,
And you can make it beat slow.
You make me smile,
And you can make me cry.
You make me feel bliss,
And you can make me feel hell.
You bring me up,
And you bring me down.
You do something to me.

LILLIAN VILLARRUEL

What we can't have

The way you ignore me and pretend not to care,
Why does that keep me around?
i find it infuriating,
yet slightly sexy.
There was something about you.

Tables have turned

The day i forgave you,
i was no longer your prisoner.
Now it was you who would suffer from guilt
For the rest of your life.
You were my prisoner now.

Hope

Press your lips against mine softly,
Let the warmth run through my veins
And bring me back to life because i'm dead inside.

Just friends

You and i will never be,
i know that don't you see.
But it doesn't mean i wont wonder
What it would be like to be yours.
i have no right to feel anger or jeal-
ousy i feel for her.
But i still can't help but wonder,
Why her and not me?
Every time you don't call
Or when you don't respond,
Lets me know that you and i will never be.

LILLIAN VILLARRUEL

While i waited for a new heart,
i borrowed a loner.
Mistreated, and forgotten,
But it got me around.

HURTING HEART

Your absence tasted sour
As tears ran down my face,
i missed you so much.

When i lay in bed,
i wonder if you're thinking of me.
i'm filled with anxiety wishing you'd call or text.
All i wanted was your attention.

The way you never fought for me,
The way you never looked at me,
The way you never cared if i was around or not.
That's where i found my answers.

You never really wanted me when you had me.
i can still remember how that pain felt.
It felt like my heart was sinking,
And i couldn't catch my breath.
i never understood why you never wanted me
until i finally decided to move on.
It took seeing me with someone else to hurt you.
i never understood why that was the most
satisfying yet horrible feeling at the same time.

Not yet

i pushed everyone away because they
needed something from me
i couldn't give them...
love.
How could i love them with this broken heart.
i didn't even love myself.

LILLIAN VILLARRUEL

i've been searching for something my whole life.
i have no idea what it is,
but i know i'm meant for something more.
Something out there is waiting for me,
It calls me and i can feel its energy.
i wish i could just find you.

Anxiety

My thoughts are so loud
i can hardly rest.

Coping

Nights like these i just wish you were here.
i lost my best friend, my soul mate.
Just laying there with you doing
nothing made me feel ok.
Just feeling your presence let me know i was loved.
i hope you know it was always you.

The destroyed

By the time you left me,
i had become just like you.
i never treated anyone from there on out
with the love and respect they deserved,
because none of them were worth it.
No one else mattered.
i had wasted all my love on you.
i just wish i knew how to get it back.

i don't want the memories,
i don't want them because they hurt so much.
i suffered my whole life,
searching for love i yearned for as a child.
i needed it badly and when i finally found it,
it was ripped away from my arms.
i don't understand.

HURTING HEART

There will come a time where i
Must stop blaming you for everything.
i just don't know where to begin,
you turned my world upside down
and it's been hard to see straight.

Why now?

You're too late.
All i ever wanted was you.
i fought so long and hard for us.
i just don't get why you never cared
until it was too late.
i'll never understand it.

Hindering feelings

i left you long ago,
but i have yet to take a deep breath
and feel the freedom.
i still feel the hurt, the love, the pain and the joy.

Listen carefully

i miss you,
but not this you.
i miss the person you used to be.
You used to love me.
i just wish you'd come back.
But then again, even if you did
i guess things just wouldn't be the same.

The pain i feel

Tell me,
When your body is pressed against mine,
Do you feel the pain i feel?
Do you feel the heat inside me of
the memories i have burned?
The wounds i have tried to cover up by
having your body pressed against mine.
Just save me please.

LILLIAN VILLARRUEL

How could you

What we had,
Is something i'll never be able to have again.
You hurt the most.

Insecure

i felt like i was never good enough,
never pretty enough.
Never strong enough.
You've been looking at me with those tired eyes.
Please…. just get some rest.

LILLIAN VILLARRUEL

Strength hurts

Why is it that strength hurts?
It took me strength to finally leave you.
It takes all my strength to not talk to you every day.
It takes all my strength not to
imagine what could have been
It takes all my strength to be strong.
My strength hurts.

Torture

Sometimes i'd just be there thinking.
Thinking about you talking to her and having fun.
Like you used to do with me.
i'm filled with this loneliness that hurts so
much, i feel like everyone else can see it.

Torn

i was afraid.
Afraid because i felt alone while having you.
You touched me but i never felt your love.
Despite that i still couldn't leave you.
Even though i've never felt more alone
while having you by my side.

Trying to steer clear

i was a fool,
i tried to forget.
So it tried to come back stronger.
i let the darkness back in.
but i have walked this path many times before,
i had it so well memorized that i
could walk it with eyes closed.
Forgive me for i was weak.
Here in the darkness i knew myself.
But it wasn't my home anymore.
i only needed to reflect.

Mirage

Masking emotions with a person's body.
Having the feeling of being in love,
When it's merely lust.
Confusion strikes and i forget who i am.

Sweet nothings

Where do you think you're going?
i've been robbed.
Someone stop them.
They filled my heart with hopes and
dreams, then ran away with it.

What you can't have

It wasn't until someone else started
to take interest in me,
That you were afraid to lose me.
That's when you knew everything i was capable of.
You were afraid i'd see you meant nothing at all,
And that soon you would be nothing
but a distant memory.

Dreaming with my eyes open

i was creating a world that i always imagined,
while trapped with you.
One day i will leave you,
And find what has been calling me,
i can already hear it.

The rage brought you power,
A sense of purpose in the relationship.
It was like a high for you.
But when tears ran down my face, the guilt would eat you up.
So, you'd hold me
And sadly, that gave me a sense of belonging.
Anything was better than to be alone.

HURTING HEART

The problem was,
You only loved me when you were lonely.
Free falling into the loneliest place of your heart,
That's where you kept me.
The place where you have forgotten to put all
your love.
Eagerly waiting each day in hopes the owner
would come home.
i saw your pain, i saw your scars, i felt your hurt.
But you never bother to take the
love i lay in between.

LILLIAN VILLARRUEL

One day,
Our souls will meet again.
Maybe now just wasn't their time.
Meet me at the same place, in years to come.
i promise i will find you
and when i do, my heart will whisper
"i remember you, do you remember me?"

HURTING HEART

i have been living in a burned paradise and calling it
home.
i always dreamt of something more.
But i let my childish fears hold me back.
You were with me,
But i had been alone all along.

LILLIAN VILLARRUEL

An ache for distant places

i long for a place i'm afraid does not exist here.
i hope for a feeling i've never felt.
i miss things i've never had.
And the one thing i am certain
of is i don't belong here.

HURTING HEART

You plucked each and every single one of my
beautiful pedals,
Till i was only left with thorns.
Forcing me to embrace my hurt and
learn to love every scar on myself.

You've stumbled into the wrong path,
you fell and it hurt so hard that
you couldn't get up because no one taught you how.
i wish somehow, someway, i could've... i wish i still could save you.
i miss you so much.
my soul, it whispers to yours in the stillness of the night.
i am still here.... i will be your light.
please, just always remember me as i remember you.
i will see you again one day.

HURTING HEART

i was tired and craved nothing more but to fall
asleep in your arms,
but you'd hardly ever come home.
And when you did it felt more
lonely than ever before.

Losing hope

i've had too many moments that didn't last forever. maybe for some people, nothing lasts forever and moments are all they have to live by.

HURTING HEART

you filled me with false hope and lies.
after i began to catch on and still decide to stay,
it was like being with you was
playing Russian roulette.

i wish you would've never lied.
i know i said i could move past it,
but it still hurts every time i remember
and now i question everything about us.

HURTING HEART

floating in darkness,
i wonder what could have been.
i miss something i've never had.
how is it possible to miss the unknown?

LILLIAN VILLARRUEL

Although i only held you for a moment,
i held your life,
and that'll give me love for a lifetime.
i don't blame you for not staying,
i know the world can be scary, i don't like it out
here much either.
But i find peace in knowing that
you will never know fear,
you will never know pain,
and you will only have felt the radiant overflowing
love i felt for you.
i will carry you in my heart until i can
carry you in Heaven my love.

HURTING HEART

Tony

sweet brother of mine,
it's been time after time
and still i miss you so.
i have peeked into your soul,
and heard your cry.
i know deep down you're in there somewhere,
and this isn't the life you imagined.
if i could pull you back up i would,
for i've tried,
but it almost seems impossible
your hurt is so heavy,
i can hardly pick it up on my own.
i love you,
i'd give anything to help you begin anew.

LILLIAN VILLARRUEL

orange skies leave glitter in your eyes,
but they've been covering up all your lies.
my heart hurts, so my mind forgets,
which just fills me with regrets.
i'm questioning things,
while tryna tie my heart to strings.
i've come to realize,
that you've been dressed in disguise.
it hurts, but it's better than not knowing
because love had already stopped flowing.

Old Habits

i must admit i have a habit.
For i fall entirely way too hard and way too fast.
Must have a little something to do with my past.
Or the lack of love i desire vast.
For i yearn for this love and affection
Because all i ever wanted was attention.
Or maybe it was the love i couldn't
see in my reflection.
Patience has become the biggest virtue,
All i want is a clear view
And to begin anew.

LILLIAN VILLARRUEL

arresting the innocent

after all the love and effort i gave
our relationship. it failed....
but yet still, even without you it's me who's
struggling to be happy with someone else.
while i watch you have the time of your life.
even though you were the broken one it's
me who's suffering for your mistakes.

Infidelity

You cheated, i stayed.
But in that moment my heart packed up and left.
My mind floated away into
thoughts of you holding her,
Squeezing her, laughing, hugging, smiling, playing.
You tell me to get over it already.
But i want her out of my home.. out of my mind.
Don't you dare ever do this to me again i tell you!
You say "baby its been months now!"
But i say "this is healing!"
i arrange my body on a platter and offer it to you
But how dare you come to me hungry while
you've already had a full serving elsewhere.
It'll take time they say
But how much time i ask?
Because days go by and months
go by and still she haunts

Me in my thoughts.
i see her in your eyes when you're looking at me.
i hate you.
She is a disease that is causing
me cancer in my brain.
Laying with you but thinking to myself
That somewhere out there, there
is love still waiting for me.
Hoping that love will send
someone to hold my hand
While i learn to love the scars on
my body that i created
From ripping you out of my life.
But that love will never find me.
Because i stay with you..
Because i'm too afraid to be alone.
Because you took away my ability
to be whole all by myself.

HURTING HEART

You cheated
And because i couldn't bear the thought of being without you, i stayed.
But the problem was, i wasn't the only one who stayed.
Thoughts of her lingered and she tainted my home in your heart.
Questions of you and her flood my mind.
Questions that i know i do not want answered
But i ask anyway.

LILLIAN VILLARRUEL

You have ripped me open and gutted me out.
i have no tears left to cry.
i have become numb to your pain you tell me is love.
My insides cry and scream
As you feed me more lies,
Feast on my body as you think of her,
Utter names in your sleep that aren't mine.
Why do i stay?
Better yet, why do you keep me?

the key under the mat

i trusted you enough to let you in. i broke down my wall for you and became vulnerable…i used to leave the key under the mat for you. but now that door is closed. it's time to start a new chapter.

Awakened

i pressed my hands against the door,
Afraid to open it.
Afraid to see what has always been.
i finally found the key and there i stood frozen.
What lies behind would awaken my slumber.

About Lillian Villarruel

FIRST TIME SELLING author Lillian Villarruel published her 1st book titled Hurting Heart at the age of 28 in 2019 with publisher 13th & Joan. She began writing as a hobby around the age of 9. After keeping journals and diaries as an outlet for depression, she slowly transitioned to writing poetry. Writing poetry helped her grow and transform from within, and gave her a powerful tool to channel what yearned to be seen and released. After surviving a traumatic childhood and a toxic violent relationship lasting a little over a decade, she set a goal for herself to publish a book by the age of 30 and she accomplished it. Still writing, poetry continues to be her goal.

www.ingramcontent.com/pod-product-compliance
Lightning Source LLC
Chambersburg PA
CBHW052050070526
44584CB00017B/2116